# Max Planck: The Life and Legacy of the Influential German Physicist Who Pioneered Quantum Theory

## By Charles River Editors

## About Charles River Editors

**Charles River Editors** provides superior editing and original writing services across the digital publishing industry, with the expertise to create digital content for publishers across a vast range of subject matter. In addition to providing original digital content for third party publishers, we also republish civilization's greatest literary works, bringing them to new generations of readers via ebooks.

Sign up here to receive updates about free books as we publish them, and visit Our Kindle Author Page to browse today's free promotions and our most recently published Kindle titles.

# Introduction

## Max Planck

"Science cannot solve the ultimate mystery of nature. And that is because, in the last analysis, we ourselves are a part of the mystery that we are trying to solve." – Max Planck

There are many feel-good fictitious stories surrounding history's most brilliant minds. Among the most widely circulated, but now debunked tales, also referred to as "copypasta," is centered on none other than Albert Einstein. This online fable, which began its rounds in emails as early as 1999, recounted a conversation between a clearly learned, yet conspicuously close-minded professor and a cautious contrarian of a student.

There are generally two versions of this tale. In the first, the professor concludes that God is evil simply on account of the existence of evil in this world. Then, however, the professor is countered by a student who stumps him with his own philosophical ramblings. "Evil does not exist, sir, or at least it does not exist unto itself. Evil is simply the absence of God. It is just like darkness and cold...Evil is the result of what happens when man does not have God's love present in his heart."

In the other version of this tale, the atheist professor seeks to dismiss the existence of God with the concept of sight – one could not see God, so, therefore, He did not exist. The student then boldly rises from his seat and poses the following question to his classmates: "Have you ever seen our professor's brain?" When the rest of his peers remained silent, the student presents this follow-up: "Have you ever felt or heard our professor's brain?" Once again, the class says nothing, and it is then that the student triumphantly declares, "It is quite obvious that our professor has no brain."

In both versions, the tale ends with a climactic reveal of the student's identity: Albert Einstein. Today, this internet fable has turned into something of a rather hackneyed running gag in the online universe, mostly used as a sarcastic response to outlandish and obviously concocted stories presented as fact.

Another lesser-known, but similarly fascinating internet parable packaged as a whimsical, yet educational anecdote revolves around an equally esteemed peer, if not mentor of Albert Einstein. This one is about Max Planck, hailed by many as one of the fathers of quantum mechanics.

The story is said to have unfolded some time during Planck's national lecture tour in Germany in the autumn of 1918. An unnamed chauffeur escorted Planck to and from the varying universities and learning institutions on his agenda, day after day. But rather than wander off for a snack, sit down with a good book, or doze off in his chair in the back of the auditoriums, the chauffeur leaned forward with a keen ear and diligently filled the pages of his journal with notes.

After about a week or so, however, the chauffeur began to grow restless, for the traveling professor had been tasked with delivering a lecture on a certain subject, thereby making his classes more or less identical. The following day, the curious chauffeur approached his employer and boldly suggested, "Professor, I have heard you give the same lecture on quantum mechanics so many times that I now know it by heart. It must be very boring for you, so for tonight, why don't we swap roles? I'll deliver the lecture and you sit in the audience and wear my chauffeur's cap."

Intrigued, Planck agreed. Prior to entering the next lecture, the pair, now disguised as the other, arranged themselves in their respective positions and proceeded with class as normal. In an era prior to mass media and the worldwide web, such a ploy could easily be executed if done correctly. And so, the chauffeur, as it turns out, would not disappoint, and he delivered the lecture like a certified professional.

The chauffeur's presentation carried on without a hitch until one of the spectators threw him off guard with a scrupulously investigated, complex question about quantum mechanics. Most would have broken down into a shivering and sweaty pile of nerves, but the chauffeur, without missing a beat, silenced him with this response: "I'm surprised that someone from the renowned city of Munich could ask such a basic question. This being the case, I will leave my chauffeur to answer it." With that, the "chauffeur" humored the professor with a meticulously detailed answer and a knowing glint in his eye.

The aforementioned tale has been relayed by some of the modern era's most gifted intellectuals and entrepreneurial powerhouses, including Charlie Munger, a business partner of Warren Buffet. The decades-old allegory is imparted not as an obscure episode in Planck's eventful life, but a story that showcases the difference between a pretentious, shallow understanding of a given subject ("chauffeur knowledge") compared to an actual, in-depth comprehension of the subject, known as "Planck knowledge." The world, they say, is overflowing with fame-hungry politicians, television doctors, armchair experts, and other glorified fraudsters who strut about with inordinate and undeserved confidence despite having inadequate knowledge. Unfortunately, the horns these characters toot are often so clamorous that the voices of those actually armed with Planck knowledge get lost in the noise.

With this analogy alone, one can get an idea of Planck's importance, and what he was like. Planck has been remembered as the theoretical physicist whose revolutionary discovery of energy quanta and formulation of fundamental quantum theory allowed for countless others to expand on the knowledge of atomic processes. The immensity of Max Planck's legacy is difficult to condense into mere words, but this excerpt from the obituary of the fabled scientist, published in *The New York Times* the day after his death, aptly summed it up: "Max Planck was one of the intellectual giants of the 20th century, and one of the [most] outstanding intellects of all time. As father of the Quantum Theory, he ranks with the immortals of science, such as Archimedes, Galileo, Newton, and Einstein...[for it was he] who gave us a master key to the universe within the atom, to the nature of light, and radiant energy in general..."

Be that as it may, there is far more to the riveting, but ultimately tragic life of this scientist than many might expect. *Max Planck: The Life and Legacy of the Influential German Physicist Who Pioneered Quantum Theory* examines the life and work that made Planck one of history's most important scientists. Along with pictures of important people, places, and events, you will learn about Planck like never before.

## A Multifarious Mind

**Planck's signature at the age of 10**

"Whence come I and whither go I? That is the great unfathomable question, the same for every one of us. Science has no answer to it." – attributed to Max Planck

On the 23rd of April, 1858, Johann Wilhelm Planck and Emma Patzig introduced a sixth member to what would soon be their brood of seven. The name of their auburn-haired baby boy would be Max Karl Ernst Ludwig Planck, as christened on the day of his baptism in Max's hometown of Kiel. It was only shortened to Max Planck shortly after the boy's 10th birthday. Max had four older siblings – Adalbert, Hildegard, Otto, and Hermann - as well as a paternal half-brother and half-sister in their early teens named Hugo and Emma. The latter pair's mother was Johann's first wife, Mathilde Voigt.

41-year-old Johann and Emma, who was four years his junior, were hardly young when Max was born, but the new addition to the family was a welcome one. The phrase, "the more, the merrier," certainly rang true in the Planck household, but unlike many other families back in the day – and perhaps even now – financial security was not among the top items on their list of burdens. The roughly 15,000 residents or so in the small town of Kiel in northern Germany mostly dealt in the shipping trade and relevant industries, but Max was a promising descendant of an illustrious lineage of esteemed intellectuals, and as such, he lived more than comfortably in the upper echelons of German society. For starters, Johann was a respected jurist and a well-paid professor of constitutional law, Roman law, and criminal procedures at the University of Kiel, and later the University of Göttingen. Max's grandfather and great-grandfather, who instilled into the family their unshakable Christian faiths and values, had also molded innumerable minds as professors of theology and law in Göttingen.

In addition to this, many of his older relatives were pastors, historians, and scholars, and they engaged in other honorable lines of work. Among these relatives was Gottlieb Planck, Max's paternal uncle, who was a prestigious judge and one of the original drafters of the *Bürgerliches Gesetzbuch,* otherwise known as the German Civil Code. And while Max's mother, Emma, never pursued academics herself, she was a woman as intelligent as she was bubbly, learning much from her accountant father. Moreover, she was well-liked by Johann's colleagues and peers, and mingled well with their wives.

The earliest years of Max's childhood were spent at the Plancks' handsome multi-story manor at Küterstrasse 17. Although the Planck children were privileged to say the least, with an army of nannies, servants, and even a personal chef at hand to cater to their every want and need, Johann and Emma ran a relatively strict household, one defined by rules, moderation, and modesty. Expectedly, education was to be among the children's highest priorities, but they were not to take precedence over the values of honesty, humility, generosity, and justice.

The Planck children were raised to respect but differentiate the institutions of church and state. This was an attitude that would now most likely be branded as "positive neutral," or, as described by Don Closson and Robin Riggs in the article "Church and State," assuming "that both religious structures and the state possess a certain degree of sovereignty over their respective domains...[with] certain rights and responsibilities [that] should be free to operate without interference from the other." Max would go on to absorb his parents' conservative political views, but after incorporating his parents' values and his own brand of liberalism, he was later classified as a "republican of reason."

It was perhaps, in hindsight, Max's trained attitude towards church and state that led him to seek out a balance between science and religion. On this note, while the open-minded Max embraced all religions, celebrating both the similarities and differences amongst the various faiths, he was himself a devout Christian, and he attended weekly Masses with his family at their local Lutheran church. Max later reflected upon the significance of his faith: "Religion represents a bond of man to God. It consists in reverent awe before a supernatural Might, to which human life is subordinated and which has in its power our welfare and misery. To remain in permanent contact with this Might and keep it all the time inclined to oneself, is the unending effort and the highest goal of the believing man. Because only in such a way can one feel himself safe before expected and unexpected dangers, which threaten one in his life, and can take part in the highest happiness – inner physical peace – which can be attained only by means of strong bond to God and unconditional trust to His competence and willingness to help."

One of the first episodes that inspired Max's need for "[safety] before expected and unexpected dangers" came around the age of 6. The melodious clopping of horse hooves against the cobblestone paths and the chatter amongst the fair ladies in straw hats and toting parasols were characteristic of a usual summer's day in Kiel. In 1864, however, the sleepy town was shaken awake by the din of marching soldiers, barking orders, and general confusion, which many residents believed portended an impactful, yet somber life inadvertently marred by the perils of war. Europe had long been embroiled in political turmoil, so discourse about military conflicts and diplomatic disagreements were hardly unusual.

Still, the sight of Bismarck's Austrian and Prussian troops stationed in his hometown at the height of the Danish-Prussian War, which had recently been annexed by King Wilhelm of Prussia, was young Max's first introduction to violence. Max's perception of war, though soon to be a destructive source of personal agony, was complex. In March of 1864, the six-year-old joined the throng of townspeople gathered at the local harbor. Like many of the young children in attendance, a bright-eyed Max peered up at 11 mighty vessels of the Baltic fleet, filled with a sense of wondrous awe. His older brother, Hermann, would give his life for his country during the Franco-Prussian War in 1870, and at least initially, Max felt "at one with the heroes who sealed their true love for the fatherland with their own blood."

On the other end of the spectrum, with age, his views on war in general evolved. The peaceable but patriotic soul was aware of the irreversible ruination and chaos brought about by war, but at the same time, he understood its necessity. When he was older, he discussed patriotism at length, saying, "Symbol of pride and honor of a famous regiment is its flag. The older it is, the higher counts its value. And its bearer considers to be his highest obligation not to let it under any conditions in lurch, he is ready to cover it in the case of need with his body, and if necessary, to [sacrifice] even his life for it. And nevertheless, the flag is just a symbol, a piece of motley cloth. Enemies can steal it, dirty, or tear it. But he will not in any case destroy the higher, which the flag stands for."

Following in the footsteps of his siblings, Max was enrolled in a local elementary school, kicking off his educational career. In addition to the formal schooling, the Planck children spent afternoons and weekends in the company of a tutor, brushing up in advance on academic or religious subjects and honing creative pursuits. This remained the arrangement throughout his elementary school years until 1867, three years after his memorable encounter with the Prussian troops.

Some chroniclers theorize that the stability of his education was threatened by the waning security and increasing unpredictability of daily life in the region, engendered by decades of protests and uprisings concerning the dwindling posts and salaries in the textile industry. The Planck family's purse strings were anything but tangled, but they were discouraged by the spike in food prices as a result of unproductive harvests, as well as the tensions it augmented. Bearing this in mind, Johann dismissed the staff of his estate in Kiel, packed his belongings, and uprooted his family to Munich that spring. Other chroniclers insist these were minor factors at best, and that it was most likely the availability of the new, higher-paying post of university rector at the Ludwig Maximilian University of Munich that attracted him to the large, bustling city 500 miles away from Kiel.

Whatever the case, it was in Munich in May 1867 that Max, now 9, began his secondary school studies at the Ludwig Maximilian Gymnasium, a reputable learning institution for academically gifted students. Context clues suggest that Max was indeed an insightful and able child, and while he performed more than adequately in school, few foresaw the groundbreaking scientific achievements he would one day accomplish. The quiet and likeable child was quite fond of his schoolbooks, regularly placing between third and eighth place in his class, but his academics, for the most part, took a back seat to his devotion to catechism, conduct, and creative talents. His instructors' impression of him was succinctly captured in Max's school report from 1872: "[Max is] justifiably favored by both teachers and classmates...and despite having childish ways, he has a very clear, logical mind. Shows great promise."

Sharp as he was, the interest Max showed in music, literature, linguistics, and theology far surpassed the passion he showed for academic fields associated with mathematics, science, and logic. Interestingly enough, this remained unchanged until the latter part of Max's secondary school years. Many, including Max himself, credited one instructor in particular with kindling the young man's dormant ardor for science. This was Herman Müller, a popular mathematics professor known for weaving physics into his lessons. Max's description of Müller, recalled with much affection, is further proof of the imprint the professor left in his life: "[Müller] was a middle-aged man with a keen mind and a great sense of humor, a past master at the art of making his pupils visualize and understand the meaning of the laws of physics."

It was one specific concept, first presented to Max during one of Müller's lectures, that sparked his fascination with the labyrinthine world of physics. This concept was the "absolute nature of the law of conservation of energy," otherwise known as the primary law of thermodynamics. To illustrate this, Müller related a story about a bricklayer who was in the process of hoisting a heavy stone brick unto the roof of his house. All the energy expended by the bricklayer, Müller explained, was housed in the stone block on the rooftop for an indefinite amount of time. The brick's conservation of energy would only be animated decades, or even centuries later, when it tumbled back to the ground. As an "absolute law of nature," such an occurrence was as impartial as it was inescapable, meaning that it was not influenced by the bricklayer's choice of building material or construction method. The only determining factors, Müller concluded, were the brick's height and weight. Max later recalled that he sat there mesmerized, "absorbing [the lecture] avidly, like a revelation." And just like that, he was hooked.

Despite his initially moderate performance in these subjects, it appeared that Müller spotted a spark he had rarely seen in his students. Pleasantly surprised by Max's sudden influx of questions and unconventional, but thought-provoking theories, Müller took it upon himself to sharpen the child's promising mathematical skills, and he provided the pupil with supplementary lessons in mechanics and astronomy after school hours. The patient professor not only heightened Max's understanding of mathematics and physics, but also taught him how to better break down and envisage the laws of physics in his mind, a holistic, yet essential tool utilized by many of history's greatest physicists.

From that point forward, Max's obsession with the subject progressively flourished. Johann further indulged his son's newfound interest by purchasing him various books on physics and the relatively new field of thermodynamics, which only began to gain traction in the early years of the 1800s. Max buried his nose in these books, primarily the publications of Benoit-Pierre Emile Clapeyron, Sadi Carnot, Hermann Helmholtz, Julius Robert Mayer, William Thomson, James Prescott Joule, and Rudolf Clausius, amongst others.

He is said to have been especially attached to the works of the German mathematician and physicist Rudolf Clausius, who first gained prestige with his reaffirmation of Carnot's principle, the Carnot Cycle, a heat theory that identifies the maximum efficiency of heat engines based on the figures of its hot and cold temperature reservoirs. It was through Clausius' work that Max received his first introduction to entropy and the second law of thermodynamics, as well as the so-called "virial theorem" for heat. Cornell University supplies this definition of the theorem: "[The theorem] states that, for a stable, self-gravitating, spherical distribution of equal mass objects (stars, galaxies, etc.), the total kinetic energy of the objects is equal to minus ½ times the total gravitational potential energy. In other words, the potential energy must equal the kinetic energy, within a factor of two."

Clausius

# Carnot

Meanwhile, Max found himself unable to detach himself from music, his first love in life. Presumably, Johann and Emma would have preferred to see their children chase after academic or theological careers, which could prolong the family's venerable legacy, but as ardent advocates of "*Bildung*," they wholeheartedly urged their children to further build their characters and stimulate their minds with nature, culture, and various creative arts. The vibrant city of Munich, famed for its artists, wordsmiths, and its proximity to picturesque landscapes, provided the Planck children with the perfect opportunity to spread their wings.

Max very much enjoyed the lengthy strolls, hikes, and nature excursions that the family regularly embarked on in the Upper Bavarian mountains and countryside. It was during these serene, but mentally and physically fulfilling dances with Mother Nature that the young man enhanced his values of forbearance, and more importantly, his ability to assess situations and overcome obstacles with a cool head. This was a technique that Max would apply to all his future undertakings.

Above all, he adored music, and, for the better part of his youth, it was as much a passion as it was an escape. The local music scene of Munich helped the naturally musical young man to master his craft. He possessed the prized gift of perfect pitch, as is commonly the case with the mathematically inclined, and relied on his natural talents to learn the piano, organ, and cello. His unequaled affinity with pitch was supposedly so potent that it almost physically pained him to sit through concerts, for even the most trivial mistakes were like grating nails on a chalkboard to his sensitive ears. He was also a trained vocalist, specializing in soprano, and was a member of the school and church choirs for several years. He even composed numerous original songs and operas, such as *Die Liebe im Walde*, or "Love in the Forest," and was fond of putting his own spin on beloved classics.

Music was far more than an extracurricular interest for his other work. In fact, it was a tool that instilled in him the power of discipline, and music demonstrated to him the fruitful results of hard work and endurance. As a dedicated devotee of the legendary Austrian pianist Emil von Sauer, Max made it a point to live and breathe by his creed. He dutifully performed Sauer's "Pischna Exercises," which were essentially technical pieces designed to train the flexibility of his fingers, and practiced for hours on end following a strict schedule, all to improve upon his skills of concentration.

**Emil von Sauer**

Alas, it soon became abundantly clear to Max around his 16th birthday that music as a career choice was a distant dream. He was a concert-grade musician, but he excelled only in covers, and though he would go on to author a few operettas, he found himself wrestling with creative blocks and unable to complete original pieces in a timely manner. Even more pressing was the fact that his love for music was slowly, but surely being eclipsed by his interest in physics.

## Choosing a Path

"It is not the possession of truth, but the success which attends the seeking after it, that enriches the seeker and brings happiness to him." – attributed to Max Planck

Shortly after his 16th birthday, Max graduated from the Ludwig Maximilian Gymnasium, and upon passing the *Abitur* (an obligatory entrance examination to university), he was enrolled in the University of Munich by the spring of 1874. Thoroughly energized by the admission, the young university student vowed to buckle down and rise up to the challenges, but he was slapped in the face by another sobering dose of reality. When Max confided in his physics professor, Philipp von Jolly, his intentions to pursue theoretical physics, the jaded instructor dismissed him with the swiftness of a vicious volleyball spike. Professor Jolly commended the student for his enthusiasm with an air of condescension in his voice, but he assured Max that there was no more untrodden ground left in the field to explore thanks to the efforts of Isaac Newton and James Clerk Maxwell, as well as the existing extensive research on thermodynamics. He asserted, "In this field, almost everything is already discovered, and all that remains is to fill a few holes." Mathematics, medicine, or some other general field of science, concluded the professor, would be a far safer choice.

**Philipp von Jolly**

**Newton**

Consequently, Max was deeply conflicted. Upon mulling it over, he approached a high-ranking professor in the university's music department and sought consultation from him. Much to his disappointment, the pompous professor gave him only this curt response, paired with a snide wave of his hand: "If you have to ask, do not choose music."

Rather than crumble, Max slept on it, and after heeding the steadfast certainty in his gut, he ultimately chose to defy his professor's warnings. Had he listened to the well-intentioned, but faulty cautioning of Professor Jolly, he would have never become the first scientist to refute the laws laid down by Newton. Indeed, Jolly's lack of faith in Max was amiss in more ways than one, because not only would he contradict scientific laws previously regarded as canon, he would also bridge classical physics and modern quantum physics.

Max elaborated on this pivotal decision in his life many years later: "[My] original decision to devote myself to science was a direct result of the discovery...that the laws of human reasoning coincide with the laws governing the sequences of the impressions we receive from the world about us; that, therefore, pure reasoning can enable man to gain an insight into the mechanism of the [world]...[The] outside world is something independent from man, something absolute, and the quest for the laws which apply to this absolute appeared...as the most sublime scientific pursuit in life..."

Despite his ultimate decision, music would remain an integral part of Max's life. He filled in for the church pianist occasionally, and later, despite his hectic schedule, he found the time to educate himself on the harmonium (a free-standing keyboard and a cousin of the pipe organ). Moreover, he used the harmonium as a tool in a number of music-related experiments. In one such experiment, he gathered a group of singers and analyzed their renditions of multiple brief musical compositions to see if they defaulted to their "natural tones" instead of relying on the "equal-tempered scale" when made to synchronize with the harmonium. His findings, which indicated that the majority opted for the latter, stunned even his teacher, Hermann von Helmholtz, who had spent the bulk of his life believing otherwise. The underrated musician at heart also attempted to breathe a different kind of life into his scientific circles by establishing a "mixed choir." The vocalists, which included Otto Hahn, Rudolf Westphal, Heinrich Hertz, and other eminent scholars, met on a regular basis at his home in Berlin-Grunewald.

Following the first major crossroads of his life, Max spent roughly the next three years at the University of Munich, engrossed in mathematics and experimental physics. At this stage, there were no classes in the specific field of theoretical physics. Given Professor Jolly's attempts to dissuade Max from immersing himself in what he described as an already polished sphere with little to no room for improvement, this should come as no surprise.

Regardless, Max had no delusions about the privileges he had been granted upon admission – namely, to be in the presence of such adulated scholars – and he refused to take his tuition for granted. More often than not, he declined invitations to dine out and engage in the usual college debauchery with his classmates, instead choosing to review his notes and read up on upcoming topics on the syllabus. Whereas most promptly shuffled out of the lecture hall once class finished, Max stayed behind and bombarded his professors with questions and his own appraisals of concepts and theories.

Apart from Jolly, an acclaimed experimental physicist most renowned for his measurements of acceleration ascribed to gravity, as well as his work with the biological process of osmosis, Max studied under the German mathematicians Philipp Ludwig von Siedel and Gustav Bauer. A little over three decades prior, Seidel had introduced to the world the revolutionary analytic phenomenon now known as "uniform convergence," and the "monochromatic aberrations" now referred to as the "Five Seidel Aberrations" were also named after him. Professor Bauer, on the other hand, specialized in variation calculus and probability theory. The following is a list of some of the lectures delivered by the aforementioned professors, as gathered from numerous class notes: Gustav Bauer – *Analytische Geometrie* (Analytical Geometry), Philipp Ludwig von Seidel – *Höhere Algebra* (Higher Algebra), Philipp von Jolly – *Mechanische Wärmetheorie*

(Mechanical Heat Theory), Wilhelm Beetz – *Allgemeine Experimentelle Physik* (General Experimental Physics).

The content of these lectures principally focused on experimental physics, and perhaps surprisingly, while Max never complained about the coursework and worked assiduously to complete his assignments, it is important to note the lack of enjoyment and enthusiasm he felt when conducting hands-on experiments. This is not to say anything about Max's skills in the art of experimentation, since he was quite efficient when it came to conducting experiments, but to him there was little appeal in running experiments to reaffirm already confirmed concepts. He also disliked the field's confinement to the studies and interactions regarding atomic structure and the properties of light, heat, and energy. The philosophical side of Max much preferred to explore and challenge the more far-reaching, intricate questions of life, such as gravity, the science of time, and the genesis of the universe, all of which were posed by the world of theoretical physics. Even so, Max was grateful for the knowledge and training he acquired during his dabbling with experimental physics, for they would most definitely come handy in his future endeavors.

Chroniclers have identified other factors that may have nudged Max towards theoretical physics. Some theorize that the young man had subconsciously done so to disprove Professor Jolly's grim predictions, and perhaps even to provoke him by pursuing a field the instructor had branded a path that led nowhere. Others claim that his gradual exposure to varying minds in the same field outside of Munich aided in his decisions. It would be wrong to write off the rudimentary knowledge and skills he had picked up from his professors at the University of Munich, but that was precisely what they were, and the more time he spent in the company of celebrated physicists outside of the staff in Munich, the more it became clear that these professors' understanding of the subject was comparatively stunted. In some areas, their understanding verged on elementary.

Some claim that it was a transformative episode with Carl David Runge, a future mathematician and physicist two years his senior, that served as the spur that catapulted Max into the enigmatic world of theoretical physics. During his spring break in 1877, the soon-to-be 20-year-old Max journeyed to northern Italy with a small band of friends, which included 22-year-old Carl. There, the friends trekked across the countryside and hiked up popular mountain trails, all the while discussing mathematics, science, and philosophy, and deliberating on different equations, concepts, and theories. Max delighted in the lively educational discourse, but it was one particular conversation regarding religion and philosophy that struck a chord with him. At one point during the trip, Max and Carl stopped briefly to marvel at the rolling hills and verdant plains before them. It was then that Carl unwittingly threw him off guard by asking whether religion did more harm than good. Max had previously pondered about the implications of religious institutions, mostly in passing, but never before had such a question been posed to him so bluntly. For the rest of the trip, Max found himself harboring reservations about his traditional

Lutheran upbringing for the first time. He had always been somewhat cynical about certain aspects of his religion, mostly concerning the truth behind inexplicable miracles, but in the same breath, he named God as the "source of all matter and atoms."

After much reflection, Max determined that as flawed as religious institutions were, faith was a vital factor in one's "scientific search for the truth." As he put it, "Anybody who has been seriously engaged in scientific work of any kind realizes that over the entrance to the gates of the temple of science are written the words: 'Ye must have faith.' It is a quality which the scientist cannot dispense with." Max shed further light upon the critical and complementary connection between science and religion in a book he authored later in life, entitled *Where Is Science Going?* In it, he wrote, "The one does not exclude the other; rather, they are complementary and mutually interacting. Man needs science as a tool of perception; he needs religion as a guide to action...There can never be any real opposition between religion and science...Every serious and reflective person realizes, I think, that the religious element in his nature must be recognized and cultivated if all the powers of the human soul are to act together in perfect balance and harmony. And indeed it was not by accident that the greatest thinkers of all ages were deeply religious souls."

Max's uncovering of this "truth," thanks to Carl's existential query, apparently elevated him to such a fulfilling state of transcendence that he made it his life's work to seek out the answers of the universe, which, in a way, would bring him one step closer to God. These answers, he believed, could only be found through the study of theoretical physics. Furthermore, this shallowly charted branch of physics provided not only the logic and reasoning of the world's most powerful, intangible phenomena, it called for discipline and methodology, values that attracted him to science in the first place. The study of the order and nature of the universe, which Max was so eager to dissect, is also referred to as "*Weltanschauung.*"

**Runge**

**Planck around the age of 20**

Max and Carl spent only three semesters together, but the pair eventually became peers and remained close confidantes moving forward. The friendship itself was as organic as they came. Like Max, Carl had once contemplated tackling non-scientific fields (in his case, literature and philosophy), but ultimately he chose to undertake mathematics and physics instead. What's more, the pair shared compatible ideals and views on life, including on how to raise their children. Culture was as every bit as imperative as education to these future fathers, much the way Max himself was raised. Carl touched on his parenting tactics with his daughter, Iris, in a letter to Max decades later: "We have fallen for the same idea as you, Max, in that we have allowed Iris to be instructed for four hours a week. She is being tutored along with the daughter of my colleague, Kohlrausch, and both of the children have been happy and enthusiastic with the arrangement."

Max's time at the University of Munich was punctuated by a fleeting exodus from his education, and followed by a brief period spent in a relevant program provided by a sister school outside of the city. During the summer vacation of 1875, the 17-year-old became sick from an undisclosed illness, and his immune system was weakened to the point that he had no choice but to temporarily excuse himself from his studies. To aid with his recovery, Max was advised to slow down and refresh his mind via new surroundings, as was the norm at the time. As such,

Max traveled to Berlin in the autumn of 1876, and he spent the following year or so taking physics classes at the University of Berlin (sometimes referred to as "Friedrich Wilhelms University").

Generally speaking, Max treasured his new professors' cosmopolitan outlook on theoretical physics. His instructors, Hermann von Helmholtz, Gustav Kirchhoff, and the "father of modern analysis," Karl Weierstrass, had previously delivered disquisitions and presentations around the continent, heard by students from cities near and far. That being said, he had overly idolized his new instructors before he had actually met them, imagining them to be far more sophisticated and professional in their fields than they turned out to be. As a result, he was eventually underwhelmed by their teaching techniques. They had succeeded only in introducing him to certain theories and encouraging him to engage in further independent research, but otherwise, the experiences "netted [him] no perceptible gain."

Professor Helmholtz, for instance, was consistently ill-prepared for his lectures. He was effervescent and engaging at his best, but he was prone to losing his train of thought and rattling off on an irrelevant tangent. More alarming yet, there were times when Helmholtz appeared to be playing catch-up with the curriculum, for he habitually stopped mid-sentence so he could gloss over his books and hastily scribbled notes. The observant Max, who was something of a perfectionist, was also irked by the erroneous calculations (most of them careless) he constantly detected on Helmholtz's blackboard. It seemed to Max, as he later revealed in his autobiography, that "the class bored [Helmholtz] as much as it did us." Such an assessment was not unfounded, and with time, the number of students in Helmholtz's classes steadily plummeted. Towards the end of the semester, only three students – Max included – had bothered to make an appearance.

### Helmholtz

Helmholtz's shortcomings aside, he was Max's favorite professor at the university. Max was drawn to Helmholtz's "scientific integrity," his dazzling zest for the subject, and the kindness and consideration he exhibited towards his students' educational progress outside of the classroom. More than that, though, it was Helmholtz's passion for thermodynamics that made the professor such a magnetic figure for Max, and Helmholtz was supposedly instrumental in intensifying Max's interest in the order and relationships between heat, energy, temperature, and work. Max would continue to consult Helmholtz occasionally throughout his career.

Professor Kirchhoff, on the other hand, was the polar opposite of Helmholtz. Kirchhoff was well-groomed, punctual, and thoroughly prepared for every lecture, perhaps even to a fault. He knew his lesson plans by heart and rarely, if ever, misspoke, speaking with a controlled tone, perfect diction, and all the appropriate inflections. That was, lamentably, the problem, for Kirchhoff consequently came off as monotonous, and his lessons were dry and overly rehearsed, as if he were reciting his words from invisible cue cards. As Max himself noted, "We would admire [Kirchhoff], but not what he was saying."

**Kirchhoff**

At the end of the day, as much as Max revered the work of his many professors, he was fully cognizant of the absence of a concrete mentor or long-term, patriarchal figure throughout the extent of his educational career. "I did not have the good fortune of a prominent scientist or teacher directing the specific course of my education," Max later mused. Fortunately, this did nothing to inhibit his ambitions. "I could just as easily have become a philologist or a historian. What led me to hard science was a course of mathematical lectures which I attended at the university and which gave me an inner satisfaction and animation."

As Max's thirst for knowledge was often left insufficiently quenched by his professors in Munich and Berlin, he took the initiative to identify misconceptions and further scrutinize the gaps of mechanical heat theory and energy principles on his own. He had already heard of Clausius, having done some light reading on his work during his gymnasium years, but it was at this stage that Max immersed himself in his work. Looking back now, it could be argued the incompetence of Max's professors was a blessing of sorts, for it served as not only the bedrock of his upcoming dissertation, but the stepping stones to his future discoveries. Thanks to all the classes, Max would later refer to this phase in his life as "*Nur nach eigener Überzeugung*" ("Only when I have convinced myself").

Max returned to the University of Munich, where he completed the remaining years of his college education, in 1878. Shortly after getting back there, he picked up from where had left off, resuming his studies on mechanical heat theory and directing the better part of his attention to entropy ("the potential that's dissipated or lost whenever a natural process takes place") and the second law of thermodynamics. He was so sold on the "absolute nature" of said law that he made it the subject of his doctoral dissertation, which he entitled *"Über den zweiten Hauptsatz der mechanischen Wärmetheorie"* ("On the Second Law of Thermodynamics"). This was the very dissertation that would soon earn him his diploma, as well as the glittering title of *summa cum laude.*

First and foremost, Max broke down the essentials of the second law, most notably that it is impossible to "turn heat into mechanical work with 100% efficiency," and illustrated how Clausius and Irish mathematical physicist and engineer William Thomson had attempted to better conceptualize and contextualize the law in question. The universe, they claimed, was naturally "active," meaning that if the distribution of energy went haywire or was even slightly out of position, thermodynamic force is instantly created to remedy the inconsistencies.

This law is evident in many areas of the physical world, like the mechanics of a steam engine, for example. Inside of an activated engine are repetitively moving pistons and cycling cranks – essentially, one type of work transforming into another at the expense of "waste heat." While "incoherent work" (referring to its fiery, "bouncing" atoms) can be produced from "coherent work" (atoms that were previously balanced and in working order), Max reaffirmed that the reverse was impossible. Such a process can be likened to hopelessly expecting cookie crumbs to piece back together without any external help. This, Max deduced, meant that engines and other similar machines were "fundamentally unbalanced" to begin with, and he summed this up in the following excerpt in his thesis: "It is impossible to construct an engine which will work in a complete cycle, and produce no effect except the raising of a weight and cooling of a heat reservoir."

David Darling, who authored *Max Planck and the Origins of Quantum Theory,* described the significance of the second law: "Whereas the first law of thermodynamics deals with things that stay the same, or in which there's no distinction between past, present, and future, the second law gives a motivation for change in the world, and a reason why time seems to have a definite, preferred direction...The second law, in its original form, states that the world acts spontaneously to minimize potentials, or equivalently, to maximize entropy."

To Max, the second law was a tool that would allow him to navigate and find the reasoning behind the universe's mysteries. Above all, the upcoming university graduate was most curious about the passage of time, as well as the universe and nature's inability to move in reverse. Such a fate, argued Max, was sealed by the absolute nature of the entropy law. This was the notion that would one day lead to the development of the thermodynamics law, also known as "Nernst's theorem," coined by chemist Walther Nernst in 1906 and finalized in 1912.

"Teaching the Third Law of Thermodynamics," a physics review authored by A. Y. Klimenko, highlights the link between the Planck formulation and the Nernst theorem: "The most common formulation of the third law of thermodynamics belongs to Max Planck...When temperature falls to absolute zero, the entropy of any pure crystalline substance tends to a universal constant (which can be taken to be zero); $S \rightarrow 0$ as $T \rightarrow 0$. Entropy selected according to $S = 0$ at $T = 0$ is called absolute. If S depends on $x$, then $x$ is presumed to remain finite...The Planck formulation, in fact, necessitates validity of two statements of unequal universality: the Einstein statement and the Nernst theorem."

## The Educator

"An important scientific innovation rarely makes its way by gradually winning over and converting its opponents: What does happen is that the opponents gradually die out." – Max Planck

In October 1878, Max took the *Staatsexamen für das Höhere* (State Examination for the Higher Magisterium) and passed with flying colors, allowing him to secure a teaching certificate in mathematics and physics. Decorated with this lustrous new credential, the budding scholar skimmed his toe against the surface of the pedagogical pool for the first time. He applied for and quickly secured the post for a substitute teacher at the Maximilian Gymnasium, his alma mater, where he instructed the next generation of gifted students on mathematics and physics.

The following February in 1879, Max was summoned to appear before the university's dissertation committee and tasked with defending his paper. The board members pressed him with multiple questions regarding thermodynamics and its cardinal laws, all of which Max answered with fluidity and ease. When he was asked about the quizzing decades later, he recounted the growing realization that began to unfold within him several minutes into the interview – judging by the ambiguity and the occasional irrelevance of their questions, it appeared that the profundity of his dissertation's message had sailed well over their heads. Nevertheless, Max kept mum and breezed through the remainder of the somewhat casual interrogation.

Later that year, Max traveled about 350 miles north to Bonn, where Clausius resided. He had sent his idol numerous letters beforehand, all of which were left unanswered. Perhaps wishfully hoping that his letters (and their responses) had gotten scrambled with some other mail somewhere along the process, Max aimed to catch the great physicist in person, even if it was only for a few minutes. The fledgling physicist longed for nothing more than the chance to toss some ideas around with such a luminary, and he was itching to unload some of his own questions.

Much to Max's dismay, all attempts to reach the physics icon fell through. Clausius was a known introvert, and he had become even more reserved in his later years, presumably more so after having suffered an unspecified lasting disability during the Franco-Prussian War in 1870. Max was certainly frustrated by the failure of his mission, but he chose to respect the recluse's wishes, returning to Munich shortly thereafter.

On the 14th of June, 1880, Max tendered his habilitation thesis, which lay a level above the Ph.D. on the academic ladder, a formal requirement for all those aiming for a professorial post. Upon the submission of his paper, entitled *Gleichge wichtszustände isotroper Körper in verschiedenen Temperaturen* (Equilibrium States of Istropic Bodies at Different Temperatures), he was awarded the *venia legendi*. The thesis, in a nutshell, delves deeper into the science of thermodynamics when coupled with the concept of entropy, which he christened the principles of "*mechanische gastheorie*," or "mechanical gas theory," as well as how elastic forces responded to entities when placed in settings of different temperatures.

In autumn of that same year, the 22-year-old was appointed an unpaid lecturer of physics at the University of Munich. Such a stint was necessary if one wished to scale the pedagogical ladder. Fortunately for Max, his family could afford to have their children remain in the nest with them for as long as they would like, and they were especially understanding of the practice, considering the family history. Thus, Max continued to lodge with his parents for the next few years. The pressure of examinations and certifications relieved from his shoulders, the young physicist could now spend his evenings, weekends, and what off time he had furthering his research on entropy.

The countless hours he had clocked both on and off campus, as well as his limited social life, would eventually pay off. On the 2nd of May, 1885, Max was appointed *professor extradordinarius,* which translates into "extraordinary professor." Not only was this his first salaried post, the title granted him greater access to crucial contacts, the use of more laboratories and resources, and a wider range of courses that touched on "electricity, optics, and mechanical heat theory." Even so, the respectability of his field of choice – theoretical physics – was perceived by many in the community as a notch below experimental physics. What followed were bittersweet results, as the number of students that signed up for his classes paled in comparison to those of his colleagues. The silver lining was that this freed up his schedule for more extensive research.

Despite the novelty of Max's chosen field, the size of his classes progressively swelled, perhaps on account of his early students' word-of-mouth promotions of him outside of the classroom. Max, who took offense to many of his previous instructors' lackluster teaching techniques, learned plenty from their deficiencies, incorporating what succeeded and eliminating what fell flat. An English student by the name of James R. Partington described Max as the "best lecturer [he had] ever heard," for the charismatic professor, who knew his material inside and out, never relied on his notes, made almost no errors, and spoke with an easy confidence that kept his students riveted throughout the entirety of his lectures. Soon, his classes evolved into "standing-room lectures," meaning they were so crowded that the tardy had no choice but to listen in from the aisles or the back of the lecture hall. "There were always many standing around the room," said Partington. "As the lecture room was well-heated and rather close, some of the listeners would from time to time drop to the floor, but this did not disturb the lecture." The feeling, of course, was not completely unanimous. A few students failed to see the allure of Max's lectures, labeling him "dry and somewhat impersonal," but they were, evidently, in the minority.

As interest continued to climb, Max and the small department for theoretical physics would be rewarded with more courses. The four courses he instructed during the winter semester of 1887-1888 were *Vorträge und Übungen aus der Electricitätslehre* (Lectures and Exercises in Electricity), *Theoretische Optik* (Theoretical Optics), *Mechanische Wärmetheorie* (Mechanical Heat Theory), and *Besprechung wichtiger Literaturescheinungen auf dem Gebiete der Wärmelehre* (Discussion of Important Literary Phenomena in the Field of Thermodynamics). The following semester, his curriculum boasted six courses. It was the additional research and familiarity he achieved with these supplementary subjects that would eventually guide him towards his pioneering radiation theory. All the while, despite the fact the class numbers grew, only 20 or so would receive a diploma.

The annual salary of 2,000 marks (approximately $15,082 USD today) Max received was far from lavish, but it was adequate enough for satisfactory financial stability. While his parents understood his predicament, he was embarrassed by his failure to depart from their nest, later remarking that he felt like "a financial drain on them." Fortunately, the academic milestone he accomplished allowed him to remedy this.

On the 31st of March, 1887, Max married his long-time girlfriend from his teenage years, the 26-year-old Marie Merck. Marie, a raven-haired beauty with delicate features from Munich, was the daughter of an affluent local banker, and the sister of a former schoolmate. The newlyweds moved into a sublet apartment in Kiel shortly afterwards, where the frugal couple made a modest, but warm home for themselves. A year later, they welcomed their first child, Karl, and in the following year, a rosy-cheeked, cherub-like pair of twins named Emma and Grete. The couple welcomed a fourth child, Erwin, in 1893.

In *The Dilemmas of an Upright Man*, J. L. Heilbron characterizes Max as "an exact economist with his time." The borderline neurotic young man rose from his bed no later than 7:30 every morning, and he made certain to begin his breakfast exactly half an hour later. He started work promptly afterwards, allowing himself his first break only at noon, before returning to work. Having said that, Max, a loyal adherent of the *Bildung*, was cautious not to overwork himself, and he always allowed himself abundant time to wind down and recharge, which added to his productivity. He took it easy during the evenings, as well as on breaks between school terms, either spending quality time with the family or hosting dinner parties for his colleagues and friends. Heilborn itemized Max's typical day in the following passage: "[He kept] a rigid schedule during term – writing and lecturing in the morning, lunch, rest, piano, walk, correspondence – and equally unrelenting recreation – mountain climbing without stopping, or talking and Alpine accommodation without comfort or privacy."

Max had encouraged Runge, amongst other friends, to break tradition and allow their daughters some form of tuition. He himself, however, was still very much a product of his time, as only his sons were enrolled in formal schools and given the complete experience. University, on the other hand, was not in the cards for the twin girls, who would be schooled by tutors for a few hours a day but otherwise had their training chiefly centered on household management and domestic affairs.

Still, while the notion of female academics was to the old-fashioned Max a pleasant anomaly, he respected their tenacity, for the obstacles they were presented with were higher than their male counterparts. He agreed to take female students under his wing, and readily provided the resources they needed to complete their doctoral educations. He was supposedly especially fond of an Austrian physics student, Lise Meitner, who later went on to become the first female salaried research assistant at the University of Berlin.

**Meitner**

According to Meitner, Max was easygoing and cool-headed, and he reportedly maintained a buoyant, playful disposition outside of the classroom throughout most of his life. These characteristics heightened even more when he became a father. "Planck loved merry, relaxed company, and his home was the center of such conviviality," said Meitner. "When the invitations happened to be during the summer term, there would be energetic games in the garden afterwards in which Planck participated with downright childish glee and great adeptness. It was almost impossible not to be tagged by him. And how visibly pleased he was when he caught someone!"

Meanwhile, Max resumed his ongoing research on thermodynamics, as well as mechanical heat and gas theory. Most of his work at this time was still primarily focused on the connection between theoretical physics and general chemistry. In 1887, a few months after his marriage, he published *Das princip der Erhaltung der Energie (The Principle of Conservation of Energy)*, an exhaustive treatise that featured a historical introduction that ran 91 pages long. Around the same time, he published *Vorlesungen über Thermodynamik (Treatise on Thermodynamics)*, in which he highlighted Arrhenius' theory of electrolytic dissociation. This exposition was followed by three other articles that spotlighted the second law of thermodynamics, this time paired with the "theory of dilute solutions and thermoelectricity."

Max was finally acknowledged for his research on thermodynamics in late 1888. On the 29th of November, a little over a year after the death of his award-winning instructor, Gustav Kirchhoff, Max was named as his heir. He was appointed assistant physics professor at the University of Berlin and inherited one of the highest-ranking chairs of the newly-founded Department of Theoretical Physics, which had been established for Kirchhoff 13 years prior. Max would remain indebted to the University of Berlin's Faculty of Philosophy, for it was they, along with the help of his ex-instructor, Helmholtz, who convinced the board in his favor. A passage from Helmholtz's recommendation letter read, "Planck's papers are very favorably distinguished from those of the majority of his colleagues in that he tries to carry through the strict consequences of thermomechanics constructively, without adding hypotheses, and carefully separates the secure from the doubtful...His papers...clearly show him to be a man of original ideas who is making his own paths...[with] a comprehensive overview of the various areas of science..."

Four years later, he was promoted to *professor ordinarius*, or as defined by Merriam-Webster, "a professor of the highest rank at a German university...with control over the teaching of a subject and a share in the government of the university." It was a tenure that lasted until the 1st of October, 1926.

Max, it appeared, had finally succeeded in carving out a name for himself in this niche, but rapidly blossoming field. Shortly after his promotion, he was inducted to the *Physikalische Gesellschaft zu Berlin* (Physical Society of Berlin) and on the 11th of June, 1894, to the *Königlich-Preussische Akademie der Wissenschaften zu Berlin* (Royal Prussian Academy of Sciences in Berlin). Moreover, he was known to have attended several meetings held by the *Gesselschaft Deutscher Naturforscher und Ärzte* (Society of German Naturalists and Doctors) between 1891 and 1899. His involvement in these exclusive circles allowed him to forge friendships and academic relationships with scores of scholars in those fields, such as Ernst Pringsheim, Wilhelm Wien, Emil du Bois-Reymond, Max B. Weinstein, Adolph von Siemens, Theodor Mommsen, Wilhelm Scherer, and Carl A. Paalzow, among numerous others. He found that his most valuable connections, however, lay in the *Physikalisch-Technische Reichsanstalt,* (Physico-Technical Imperial Institute), where he rubbed elbows with the most esteemed experimental physicists, including Ludwig Holborn, Otto Lummer, and Ferdinand Kurlbaum. He also participated in discussions developed by scientists and scholars all throughout Germany and neighboring nations via mail. Ernst Lecher, Arnold Sommerfeld, Heinrich Hertz, Leo Koenigsberger, Albert Schweitzer, and the Austrian-Dutch physicist Paul Ehrenfest were just a few of his pen pals.

Sadly, despite the new connections and his growing pool of resources, Max still felt like a fish out of water. He later wrote, "In those days, I was essentially the only theoretical physicist there, whence things were not so easy for me, because I started mentioning entropy, but this was not quite fashionable, since it was regarded as a mathematical spook."

Those who had such things to say would soon be silenced.

## Swimming Against the Tide

"It is not the possession of truth, but the success which attends the seeking after it, that enriches the seeker and brings happiness to him." – Max Planck

Legend has it that it was a special commission from the German Bureau of Standards in the early 1890s that propelled Planck into the untraversed universe of quantum mechanics. With the official treasury running disconcertingly low, the bureau was desperately seeking out a way to slash costs. As such, Max was tasked with designing a new type of low-energy light bulb that would produce the brightest flare possible.

It was during Max's experimentation with various existing light bulbs that his wandering mind abruptly happened upon another unanswered question. In asking himself what it was that gave the light of these bulbs their golden-yellow glow, he seemed to sense a direct contradiction of some of the most fundamental rules of classic physics. The yellow glow, he theorized, was most likely chosen for its "easy visibility," but all heated objects were expected to emit only shorter, invisible wavelengths of radiation. This peculiar puzzle, which he later dubbed "the black-body radiation problem" before the German Physical Society of Berlin, quickly lodged itself into place as the center of his attention.

After several exasperating weeks, Max communicated his inability to complete the assignment and parted ways with the bureau. Normally, such an abdication would have gnawed away at him, but any sense of shame was thoroughly clouded by the excitement of an impending Eureka moment. At the time, Max had only expected to add an extension to an existing law of physics at most, so even he would be shocked at the coming discovery would turn his own world around.

Today, many have chalked up the light bulb story to lore, a myth has been retold time and time again with different versions to the tale. In some, Max's employer is identified as the "German Bureau of Standards," and in others, it's an unnamed energy corporation. No such bureau, however, existed; its closest equivalent was the *Physikalisch-Technische Reichsanstalt*, or the PTR.

Nonetheless, however it happened, it was during this time that Max began his research on black-body radiation. At this point in time, physicists were unable to illustrate in detail why the intensity of electromagnetic radiation expelled by black bodies, also referred to as "perfect absorbers," was determined by the frequency (which dictates the color of the light discharged) and its temperature. After roughly six years of trial and error, Max tentatively settled upon the startling conclusion that the flow of light was not constant, but that light traveled in "discreet packets" he called "quanta."

Max was initially hesitant to publish his discovery, for such a finding clashed discordantly with the established laws of physics, and the findings unraveled even many of his own beliefs on thermodynamics. Ironically, there was a time when Newton himself had pondered if light traveled in "energy packets," but his unearthing of interference patterns quickly convinced him to shun such a thought. There was no doubt, concluded Newton, that light traveled only as "a continuous wave of energy." Max's theory, which called to attention the "duality of light," asserted that light could act as both a particle and a wave, and thus could be quantifiably measured with respective devices.

Today, Max's theory is referred to as the "Planck Postulate," and it can be mathematically defined by the following equation: *"E = hv,"* with *E* representing "energy," *h* representing the Planck constant, and *v* representing the frequency. Planck's Quantum Theory can be further summarized with the following three factors:

"1. The energy of a photon is dependent on the wavelength.

2. Substances radiate or absorb energy discontinuously in the form of small packets or bundles of discrete energy...called 'quanta.'

3. Quantum in case of light is called a 'photon.'"

December 14, 1900, which marks the day of Max's trailblazing discovery, is now hailed by many as the birthday of modern quantum physics. Of course, the physicist could not have imagined the portals – or as some would say, rabbit holes – that he had created in the field, but the ripples and repercussions he had caused were not completely lost on him. Once all his work and findings were in order, Max stumbled out of his home office in such a state of giddy glee that he nearly collided with his son, Erwin, in the hall, to whom he blurted, "Today I made a discovery as important as Newton's discovery of gravity!"

Max later revealed the chaos within his mind in the days just before and after his discovery of quanta: "[I]t seemed so incompatible with the traditional view of the universe provided by physics that it eventually destroyed the framework of this older view. For a time, it seemed that a complete collapse of classical physics was not beyond the bounds of possibility; gradually, however, it appeared, as had been confidently expected by all who believed in the steady advance of science, that the introduction of Quantum Theory led not to the destruction of physics, but to a somewhat profound reconstruction..."

The discovery eventually led to the introduction of the Planck Units, otherwise known as the "Planck Scale." The general measurements are as follows: "a kilogram – the mass of a liter of water; a meter – one ten-millionth of the distance from the North Pole to the Equator; and a second – 1/86,400 of an Earth day." A century later, none other than Stephen Hawking calculated that the smallest black hole in the universe had a mass of "1 Planck mass unit, a Schwarzschild radius of 1 Planck length unit, and a half-life of 1 Planck time unit."

Following the most momentous discovery of Max's career, he continued to conduct research across various branches of sciences and help others in those fields. On top of those involved in the study of thermodynamics, he contributed to optics, physical/general chemistry, and statistical mechanics. In 1905, Max ruffled even more feathers by endorsing the controversial theories spouted by a then-lowly employee of the Swiss patent office in Bern named Albert Einstein.

The bond that developed between Planck and Einstein was more of a case of opposites attract. As spruce as he was a man of methodical routine, Max identified as a (moderate) conservative and cherished the academic career he had worked so hard to build. In contrast, Einstein was famously sloppy in dress but brilliant in mind, and he was a fierce liberal who loathed the formalities and all things associated with the excessively exclusive university culture. Still, the pair became fast friends, bound by their mutual love for music and "absolute truths," and they remained deeply intimate colleagues for the remainder of their lives.

**A 1931 picture of Planck seated next to Einstein**

Like many of Max's previous dissertations and publications, the complexity of Einstein's special theory of relativity could not be fully grasped by the scientific community. Many were suspicious about the validity of Einstein's theory, for it was, in a sense, attempting to calculate the multifaceted motions from angles that necessitated incomputable speeds. Max's biographers claim that it was his vigorous vouching for Einstein that ultimately led to the community's acceptance of the unconventional theory. Furthermore, it was Max who apparently urged Einstein to release his following five papers concerning general relativity. Max, who would later serve as chief editor for the *Annalen der Physik (The Annals of Physics),* went on to publish the literature in the nationally acclaimed scientific journal. For his part, Einstein, who worshiped the misprized theoretical physicist with equal relish, described Max's discoveries as "previously unimagined thought, the atomist structure of energy."

In 1918, Max received the acknowledgment of a lifetime when he was accorded the Nobel Prize in Physics "for the services he rendered to the advancement of Physics by his discovery of energy quanta." After some ruminating, he unveiled his thoughts on acquiring the milestone in his Nobel Lecture on June 2, 1920, saying, "For many years, [my objective] was to solve the problem of energy distribution in the normal spectrum of radiating heat. After...Kirchhoff has shown that the state of the heat radiation which takes place in a cavity bounded by any emitting and absorbing material at uniform temperature is totally independent of the nature of the material, a universal function was demonstrated which was dependent only on temperature and wavelength, but not in any way on the properties of the material. The discovery of this remarkable function promised deeper insight into the connection between energy and temperature...and so in all of molecular physics...Because [a constant in the radiation law] represents the product of energy and time...I described it as the elementary quatum of action...As long as it was looked on as infinitely small...everything was fine; but in the general case...a gap opened wide somewhere or other...That all efforts to bridge the chasm foundered soon left little doubt...In this case, the quantum of action must play a fundamental role in physics, and here was something completely new, never heard of before, which seemed to require us to basically revise all our physical thinking, built as this was, from the time of the establishment of the infinitesimal calculus by Leibniz and Newton, on accepting the continuity of all causative connections..."

By the second decade of the 20th century, Max was among the most decorated theoretical physicists in the industry. In 1912, he was appointed secretary of the Mathematics and Physics wing for the Prussian Academy of Sciences, a post he held until 1938. He later served as the president of the Kaiser Wilhelm Society for the Advancement of Science between the years of 1930 and 1937. His accomplishments were further recognized with his appointment to the Foreign Membership of the Royal Society in 1926, as well as the coveted Copley Medal two years later.

Naturally, when someone reaches the absolute pinnacle of life, there's only direction to go from there. Unfortunately for Planck, it was not a gradual descent but a tragic, rapid downfall. In 1909, his beloved wife of 22 years passed away due to complications from tuberculosis. The widower sought comfort in his children, as well as in his new wife, Marga von Hösslin. They had a son, Hermann, born in December 1911.

Any joy he experienced from having another son proved short-lived, because in 1916, he lost his oldest son, Karl, who was killed in the Battle of Verdun during World War I. In 1917, his daughter Grete suffered complications during childbirth and died shortly thereafter. In an eerie twist of fate, her twin, Emma, met the exact same fate two years later. Both of Max's grandchildren survived, but aside from them, only two of Max's children, Hermann and his son Erwin from his first marriage, remained.

By the time World War II started in 1939, many German scientists who were wary of Adolf Hitler and the Nazi regime had already relocated elsewhere, especially those of Jewish descent like Einstein. They proved to be quite prescient, but Planck, like others, found it difficult to even entertain such an impulse. The physicist unequivocally despised Hitler, but the patriotic part of him made it impossible to part with his homeland, especially in such dire times. He later explained, "I've been here in Berlin at the university since 1889, so I'm quite an old-timer. But there really aren't any genuine old Berliners, people who were born here; in the academic world, everybody moves around frequently. People go from one university to the next one, but in that sense, I'm actually very sedentary. But once I arrived in Berlin, it wasn't easy to move away; for ultimately, this is the center of all intellectual activity in the whole of Germany."

Inevitably, the Nazis saw Max as a non-aggressive, but persistent pest that threatened their "cleansing" of German academic circles. First and foremost, they took issue with the religiously tolerant scientist's refusal to filter out non-Christian values when weaving religion into his lectures. He incurred further wrath through his quiet, but unwavering support for Einstein and other Jewish physicists and scholars, so much so that he was mocked as a "white Jew" and vilified as a "bacteria carrier" in the official Nazi newsletter, *Das Schwarze Korps.* Moreover, Planck consistently voted against candidates with Nazi ties who were vying for positions in the Prussian Academy of Sciences.

Over time, Planck penned several letters addressed to Hitler himself, imploring the dictator to allow his fellow Jewish colleagues to retain their posts. Of course, the requests fell on deaf ears, and when the Nazis forcibly seized the Academy in 1938, Max surrendered his presidential post as a sign of protest.

Despite the persecution and his opposition to the Nazis, glorifying Planck would be rash. As solid as his opposition was to the Nazi principles, he made the choice to comply with various Nazi-issued regulations, and following an especially heated crackdown on Jewish academics, he demonstrably tamped down his concerns. His convenient reticence is further evidenced in this account provided by physicist Paul Elwald, a member of the Kaiswer Wilhelm Institute of Metals: "[W]e were all staring at Planck, waiting to see what he would do at the opening, because at that time it was prescribed officially that you had to open such addresses with 'Heil, Hitler.' Well, Planck stood on the rostrum and lifted his hand half high, and let it sink again. He did it a second time. Then, finally, the hand came up and he said, 'Heil, Hitler.' Looking back, it was the only thing you could do if you didn't want to jeopardize the whole Society."

In 1944, as Nazi Germany's growing woes intensified, so did Planck's personal problems. An air raid destroyed his home in Berlin that year, along with irreplaceable documents and original copies of various treatises. As it turned out, however, the destruction of virtually his entire life's work would soon prove to be the least of his dilemmas.

Max's son, Erwin, a former government official, permanently withdrew himself from the vicious arena of politics back in 1933, but upon the rise of the Nazis, he covertly reentered the arena. He was linked to numerous underground anti-Nazi campaigns, and he was even part of the secret committee that drafted a constitution that would be inaugurated following the dismantlement of the oppressive regime. In the early months of 1944, Erwin was arrested, charged as one of the conspirators behind Claus Stauffenburg's assassination attempt on Hitler, and sentenced to death.

**Erwin in 1932**

   Max was 87 at the time of his son's arrest, and he frantically composed numerous letters addressed to Heinrich Himmler and Hitler. One letter to Hitler begged the dictator to spare his son's life on account of his own career: "I am most deeply shaken by the message that my son, Erwin, has been sentenced to death by the People's Court. The acknowledgment for my achievements in service of our fatherland, which you, my Führer, have expressed towards me in repeated and most honoring way, makes me confident that you will lend your ear to an imploring [senior citizen]. As the gratitude of the German people for my life's work, which has become an everlasting intellectual wealth of Germany, I am pleading for my son's life."

   On January 23, 1945, Erwin was hanged.

   When the war came to a close months after his son's execution, Max moved what was left of his family to Göttingen, where they lived with a relative. On October 4, 1947, Max Planck's eyes fluttered shut for the very last time, at the age of 89. His body now rests in Göttingen's City Cemetery, where he is accompanied by the graves of Marga and Hermann.

The following year, the Kaiser Wilhelm Society was rechristened the "Max Planck Society" as an eternal homage to the exalted theoretical physicist and father of quantum physics. The Max Planck Society, which now consists of over 80 departments, continues to be an imposing force to be reckoned with in the world of modern science. Researchers from his namesake have since acquired an astounding collection of Nobel Prizes, including eight in chemistry, six in medicine, and four in the field of physics.

**Online Resources**

Other books about scientists by Charles River Editors

Other books about Planck on Amazon

**Further Reading**

Editors, H. C. (2017). MAX PLANCK BORN. Retrieved September 26, 2018, from https://www.historychannel.com.au/this-day-in-history/max-planck-born/

Editors, M. E. (2015, November 13). Max Planck. Retrieved September 26, 2018, from https://micro.magnet.fsu.edu/optics/timeline/people/planck.html

Editors, F. P. (2017, October 4). Max Planck Biography. Retrieved September 26, 2018, from https://www.thefamouspeople.com/profiles/max-planck-4977.php

Stuewer, R. H. (2018, September). Max Planck. Retrieved September 26, 2018, from https://www.britannica.com/biography/Max-Planck

Ferro, S. (2017, August 22). 17 Little-Known Facts About Max Planck. Retrieved September 26, 2018, from http://mentalfloss.com/article/502908/17-little-known-facts-about-max-planck

Editors, N. P. (2016). Max Karl Ernst Ludwig Planck. Retrieved September 26, 2018, from https://www.nobelprize.org/prizes/physics/1918/planck/biographical/

Editors, E. F. (2003, October). Max Karl Ernst Ludwig Planck. Retrieved September 26, 2018, from http://www-groups.dcs.st-and.ac.uk/history/Biographies/Planck.html

Editors, F. S. (2016, May 17). Max Planck. Retrieved September 26, 2018, from https://www.famousscientists.org/max-planck/

Editors, T. H. (2012). Max Planck. Retrieved September 26, 2018, from http://totallyhistory.com/max-planck/

Williams, M. (2017, January 17). Who was Max Planck? Retrieved September 26, 2018, from https://www.universetoday.com/85155/max-planck/

Editors, C. (1995). MAX PLANCK. Retrieved September 26, 2018, from https://www.cosmos.esa.int/web/planck/max-planck

Moose, C. J. (1999). Max Planck Biography. Retrieved September 26, 2018, from https://www.enotes.com/topics/max-planck

Editors, E. C. (2014). Planck, Max Karl Ernst Ludwig. Retrieved September 26, 2018, from https://www.encyclopedia.com/people/science-and-technology/physics-biographies/max-planck

Kragh, H. (2000, December). Max Planck: The reluctant revolutionary. Retrieved September 26, 2018, from https://pdfs.semanticscholar.org/7aeb/37159b682b0e5ce54cdeb2834ccb4dbcd5be.pdf

Editors, B. O. (2017). Max Planck Biography. Retrieved September 26, 2018, from https://www.biographyonline.net/scientists/max-planck-biography.html

Editors, P. U. (2012). MAX PLANCK (1858 - 1947). Retrieved September 26, 2018, from https://www.physicsoftheuniverse.com/scientists_planck.html

Rosenberg, J. (2018, April 15). Max Planck Formulates Quantum Theory. Retrieved September 26, 2018, from https://www.thoughtco.com/max-planck-formulates-quantum-theory-1779191

Yan, W. D. (2016, April 22). Who was Max Planck? Retrieved September 27, 2018, from https://daily.jstor.org/who-was-max-planck/

Editors, M. P. (2018). Family, childhood, youth. Retrieved September 27, 2018, from http://www.max-planck.mpg.de/seite03/english.html

Editors, G. (2016, February 29). Max K. E. L. Planck, Nobel Prize in Physics, 1918. Retrieved September 27, 2018, from https://www.geni.com/people/Max-K-E-L-Planck-Nobel-Prize-in-Physics-1918/6000000000632928642

Daniel, P. (2010, November 28). Max Planck On God. Retrieved September 27, 2018, from https://withalliamgod.wordpress.com/2010/11/28/max-planck-on-god/

Roman, A. (2014, July 18). Remarkable attitude of Max Planck to religion. Retrieved September 27, 2018, from http://adam.humanisti.sk/?p=133

Williamson, H. (2017, February 16). 10 Brilliant Scientists and Their Views of God. Retrieved September 27, 2018, from https://owlcation.com/humanities/10-Brilliant-Scientists-and-Their-View-of-God

Editors, A. A. (2017, May 2). Max Planck on God, Science, and Religion. Retrieved September 27, 2018, from http://doctorpence.blogspot.com/2017/05/max-planck-on-god-science-and-religion.html

Perutz, M. F. (2011). The Dilemmas of an Upright Man: Max Planck as Spokesman for German Science: Review. Retrieved September 27, 2018, from https://www.lrb.co.uk/v09/n01/mf-perutz/german-scientist

Editors, A. (2005, October 5). The Religious Affiliation of Physicist Max Planck. Retrieved September 27, 2018, from http://www.adherents.com/people/pp/Max_Planck.html

Editors, O. E. (2015, May 17). Working & Living Conditions During the Late 1800s. Retrieved September 27, 2018, from https://u.osu.edu/berlin2798ranthenau/2015/05/17/working-living-conditions-during-rathenaus-time/

Valdano, D. (2017, March 29). Entropy was Max Planck's gateway drug to Quantum Mechanics. Retrieved September 27, 2018, from https://medium.com/physics-as-a-foreign-language/entropy-was-max-plancks-gateway-drug-to-quantum-mechanics-89893641e327

Editors, S. S. (2016). Max Planck Facts. Retrieved September 27, 2018, from http://www.softschools.com/facts/scientists/max_planck_facts/1723/

Fergus, J. (2015, November 23). Max Planck and Albert Einstein. Retrieved September 27, 2018, from https://blog.oup.com/2015/11/max-planck-albert-einstein/

Editors, H. U. (2013, November 14). Max Planck's Cosmic Harmonium. Retrieved September 27, 2018, from https://www.physics.harvard.edu/node/254

Editors, M. P. (2017). Academic studies. Retrieved September 27, 2018, from http://www.max-planck.mpg.de/seite04/english.html

Ebeling, W. (2008). Max Planck on Entropy and Irreversibility. Retrieved September 27, 2018, from https://bilder.buecher.de/zusatz/23/23411/23411877_lese_1.pdf

Kubbinga, H. (2018, April). A TRIBUTE TO MAX PLANCK. Retrieved September 27, 2018, from https://www.europhysicsnews.org/articles/epn/pdf/2018/04/epn2018494p27.pdf

Shankar, A. (2014, November 29). Is the story about Max Plank and his chauffeur actually true? Retrieved September 28, 2018, from https://www.quora.com/Is-the-story-about-Max-Plank-and-his-chauffeur-actually-true

Evans, R. (2015, September 20). A lesson from German physicist Max Planck on successful investing. Retrieved September 28, 2018, from https://www.telegraph.co.uk/finance/personalfinance/investing/11874031/A-lesson-from-German-physicist-Max-Planck-on-successful-investing.html

Beck, L. F. (2018). Max Planck. Retrieved September 28, 2018, from https://www.mpg.de/8241451/max-planck-kwg

O'Reilly, T. (2005, June 21). Planck knowledge and chauffeur knowledge. Retrieved September 28, 2018, from http://radar.oreilly.com/2005/06/planck-knowledge-and-chauffeur.html

Darling, D. (2017). Max Planck and the origins of quantum theory. Retrieved September 28, 2018, from http://www.daviddarling.info/encyclopedia/Q/quantum_theory_origins.html

Keller, F. O. (2014, April 23). Ein Pianist, ein Gelehrter, ein Christ. Retrieved September 28, 2018, from https://www.zeit.de/1958/17/ein-pianist-ein-gelehrter-ein-christ

Rajput, J. (2016, October 2). What are some cool or lesser known facts about Max Planck? Retrieved September 28, 2018, from https://www.quora.com/What-are-some-cool-or-lesser-known-facts-about-Max-Planck

Editors, 3. S. (2018, May 23). Who Am I: Max Planck? Retrieved September 28, 2018, from http://blog.3bscientific.com/2018/05/23/who-am-i-max-planck/

Editors, S. N. (2014). The Early Years. Retrieved September 28, 2018, from http://www.sparknotes.com/biography/planck/section1/

Editors, S. (2018, April 25). Did Albert Einstein Humiliate an Atheist Professor? Retrieved September 28, 2018, from https://www.snopes.com/fact-check/false-einstein-humiliates-professor/

Bhargava, R. (2013, May 15). MARKETING GENIUS: THE MAN WHO MENTORED EINSTEIN. Retrieved September 28, 2018, from https://www.americanexpress.com/us/small-business/openforum/articles/how-max-planck-proved-the-greatest-marketing-lesson-of-all-time/

Editors, M. P. (2017). Politics and the state. Retrieved September 28, 2018, from http://www.max-planck.mpg.de/seite18/english.html

Closson, D., & Riggs, R. (2000). Church and State. Retrieved September 28, 2018, from http://www.leaderu.com/orgs/probe/docs/churchstate.html

Editors, D. W. (2018, June 2). Wilhelm von Planck. Retrieved September 28, 2018, from https://de.wikipedia.org/wiki/Wilhelm_von_Planck

Editors, C. U. (2011). The Virial Theorem. Retrieved September 28, 2018, from http://hosting.astro.cornell.edu/academics/courses/astro201/vt.htm

Editors, E. C. (2008). Runge, Carl David Tolmé. Retrieved September 28, 2018, from https://www.encyclopedia.com/science/dictionaries-thesauruses-pictures-and-press-releases/runge-carl-david-tolme

Editors, R. (2017, February 9). Philipp von Jolly. Retrieved October 1, 2018, from https://www.revolvy.com/page/Philipp-von-Jolly

Editors, S. C. (2018). Difference Between Theoretical & Experimental Physicist. Retrieved October 1, 2018, from https://study.com/articles/difference_between_theoretical_experimental_physicist.html

Klimenko, A. Y. (2012, August 22). Teaching the third law of thermodynamics. Retrieved October 1, 2018, from https://arxiv.org/pdf/1208.4189.pdf

Editors, M. P. (2017). Entering on a career in academia. Retrieved October 1, 2018, from http://www.max-planck.mpg.de/seite05/english.html

Editors, P. B. (2016). Max Planck (1858-1947). Retrieved October 1, 2018, from http://physicsbook.gr/index.php?option=com_content&view=article&id=121:max-planck&catid=61:physics&Itemid=113&lang=en

Liszewski, A. (2012, October 15). How Quantum Mechanics Was Born From the Need For a Better Lightbulb. Retrieved October 1, 2018, from https://gizmodo.com/5951751/how-quantum-mechanics-was-born-from-the-need-for-a-better-lightbulb

Editors, E. (2000, December 7). Just thanck Planck. Retrieved October 1, 2018, from https://www.economist.com/science-and-technology/2000/12/07/just-thanck-planck

Orzel, C. (2015, May 21). The Surprisingly Complicated Physics Of A Light Bulb. Retrieved October 1, 2018, from https://www.forbes.com/sites/chadorzel/2015/05/21/the-surprisingly-complicated-physics-of-a-light-bulb/#8f3808d4f555

Editors, T. V. (2017). Max Planck. Retrieved October 1, 2018, from https://chemistry.tutorvista.com/physical-chemistry/max-planck.html

Farmelo, G. (2017). MAX PLANCK LETTER TO HITLER DISCOVERED. Retrieved October 1, 2018, from http://grahamfarmelo.com/max-planck-letter-hitler-discovered/

Editors, O. T. (2018). Max Planck Dead; Noted Physicist, 89. Retrieved October 1, 2018, from http://movies2.nytimes.com/learning/general/onthisday/bday/0423.html

Stewart, I. (2007). *Why Beauty Is Truth: The History of Symmetry*. Basic Books.

Planck, M. (2014). *Scientific Autobiography: And Other Papers*. Open Road Media.

Weir, J. (2009). *Max Planck: Revolutionary Physicist*. Capstone.

Haven, K. F. (1999). *100 Most Popular Scientists for Young Adults: Biographical Sketches and Professional Paths*. Libraries Unlimited.

Brown, B. R. (2015). *Planck: Driven by Vision, Broken by War*. Oxford University Press.

## Free Books by Charles River Editors

We have brand new titles available for free most days of the week. To see which of our titles are currently free, click on this link.

## Discounted Books by Charles River Editors

We have titles at a discount price of just 99 cents everyday. To see which of our titles are currently 99 cents, click on this link.

Made in the USA
Monee, IL
08 September 2023